IQ BOOSTERS

Planning Guides

Brent R. Evans

IQ Boosters Planning Guides
Brent R. Evans

Copyright 2018 Brent R. Evans

Bookwise Publishing
Riverton, Utah
www.bookwisepublishing.com

Editor & Producer: K Christoffersen

Cover & Interior Design Paul Killpack and K Christoffersen
Illustrator: Tom Macris

ISBN 978-1-60645-230-1 Trade Paperback

10 9 8 7 6 5 4 3 2 1

boostingiq.com or learningsuccess.com

Version 9232018GUIDES

ACKNOWLEDGMENTS

I want to thank the thousands of children, parents, and teachers who over several decades contributed to making this book a powerful tool to increase intelligence. As a teacher, counselor, and Resource Specialist in the Cupertino School District, I researched, developed and applied the habits, activities, and games that can increase each area of intelligence. Every school day I would bring a box of research books so I could learn and apply what was in them. I tested the current level of a student's IQ and was able to retest that same student months and sometimes years later and see their IQ go up and up.

—Brent R. Evans

There is so
much to learn
and see!

Table of Contents

IQ BOOSTERS

FAMILIES CAN BOOST IQ

Thirteen Key Areas of Intelligence

If you're like most parents, you want a home that is safe and secure; one that is comfortable, interesting, and exciting with a family life full of love and care for one another, and rich relationships to build self-esteem and confidence. Only a few people fully realize they can have more—a home that can significantly promote intelligence, achievement, and success.

To do this more dramatically than ever before possible, IQ Boosters puts in your hands all the tools you need. Learn to develop in yourself and your children Thirteen Key Areas of Intelligence recognized today as vitally important for both school achievement and success in life. More than nine hundred powerful time management ideas, everyday habits, simple activities, and fun games are instantly available for you to use to your family's best advantage.

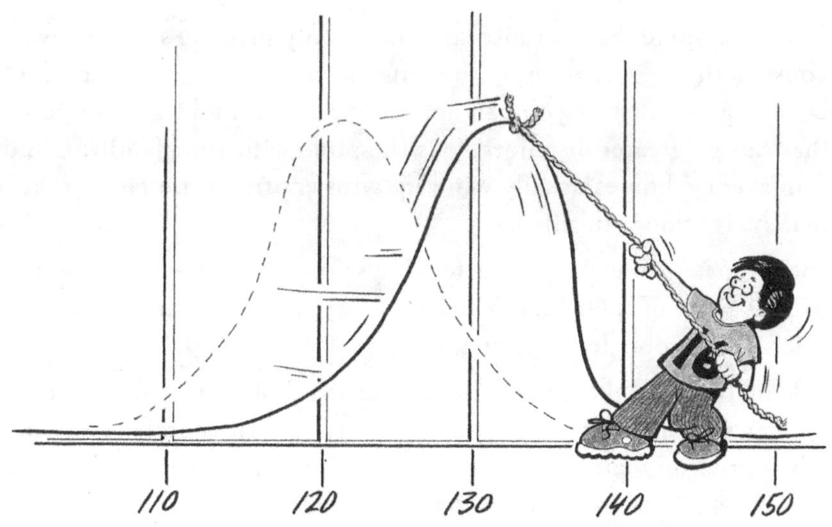

As a parent in the 21st century, it's more important than ever that you have the best tools and information related to IQ development and success than anyone else who will ever have contact with your child. No one will ever love your children more than you do; they will not have as much interest in their development and welfare. No other person or group of people will have as many key opportunities to help your children grow and develop to their fullest potential. Your power is at least four times as great as the power of any teacher or school your children will ever attend.

Building a home that can increase each family member's success is much like constructing a rocket ship. You can build an average rocket ship and expect average results, or you can add boosters and build a more powerful one that can go greater distances. It is the same with your family. Children raised in average homes usually wind up with enormous potential that, unfortunately, is seldom fulfilled.

Albert Einstein was purported to have said the average person uses only about 14 percent of their brain capacity. Why not ignite that 86 percent of potential most people leave dormant?

Back in the 60s, the great educational psychologist, Joseph McVicker Hunt, suggested that if we could better govern the encounters children have with their environments, we could substantially increase their intelligence by as much as 30 points. What a challenge!

This is important to parents because the majority of the key encounters needed to boost IQ is within their control in their own homes. IQ can be boosted by relatively simple adjustments to your everyday family patterns of living with one another. The problem for parents is that most of the relevant research is buried deep and scattered wide in university libraries in hard-to-read educational and psychological journals and papers.

Even more important, before the research can be used, it needs to be translated into practical ideas and tools that ordinary parents, often hard-pressed by many other challenges in life, can understand and apply with a minimum of time and effort.

My first attempts in translating this research some years ago were in designing learning programs called *Make It a Habit* and *Brain Builders* that appeared on Quaker's Life cereal boxes. That program was so successful that Quaker had me tour schools, and TV and radio stations across the nation. Sales of Life Cereal increased to record highs. Because of this astounding success, Quaker asked me to come up with a learning program for their King Vitaman cereal boxes. It was called the *Ask King Vitaman! I Want to Know!*

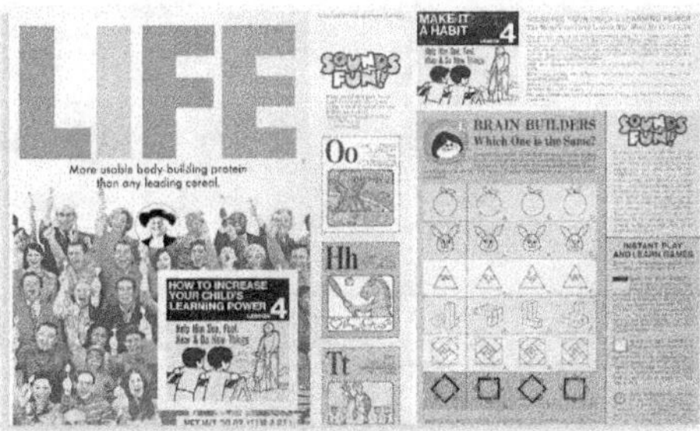

Children could write to King Vitamin (me) and ask how to do something better. This resulted in tens of thousands of letters requesting ways to learn all sorts of things better, like how to memorize or spell better. I would select one child's letter for each box series. The child's photo and letter would be printed on the cereal box and there would be games on the box to help them, and all who had one on their table, develop that skill. I prepared game sheets for each skill and Quaker sent them their own personalized games.

Now, after more than forty years of further research and development, I feel I have answered J. McVicker Hunt's challenge. IQ Boosters is a complete program to move the IQ curve higher for you and your entire family.

—Brent R. Evans

Increase IQ

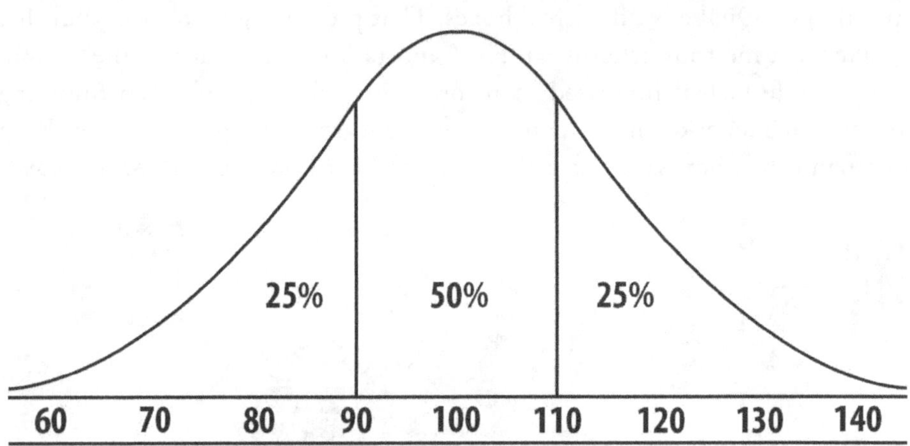

FREQUENCY DISTRIBUTION OF IQ

The *Frequency Distribution of IQ* chart is very demonstrative. Put your finger where you feel your current IQ might be. Then move it 10, 20, or 30 points to the right.

Imagine the opportunities and enjoyment that might be added to your life and what it might do for each of your children!

The average IQ of a college graduate is only 10 points higher than the average high school graduate. There is also only a 10-point difference between the average college graduate and the average doctoral graduate.

Average IQ & Educational Attainment

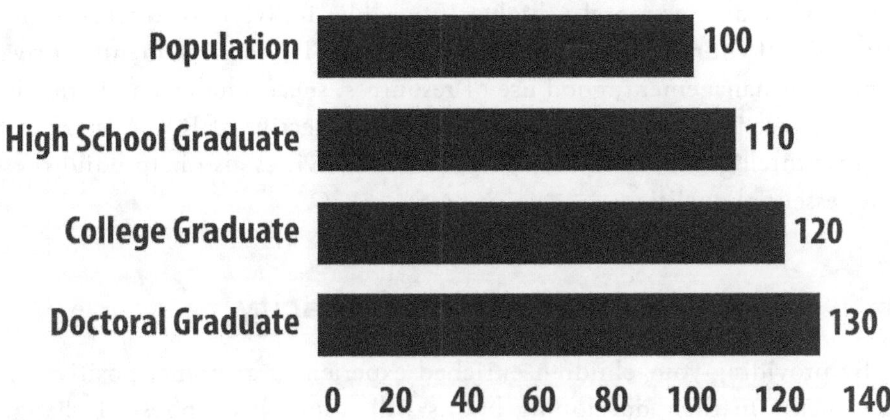

From Cronbach's *Essentials of Psychological Testing 2nd Edition*, New York, NY, Harper, 1980, p. 174

Education & Income Potential

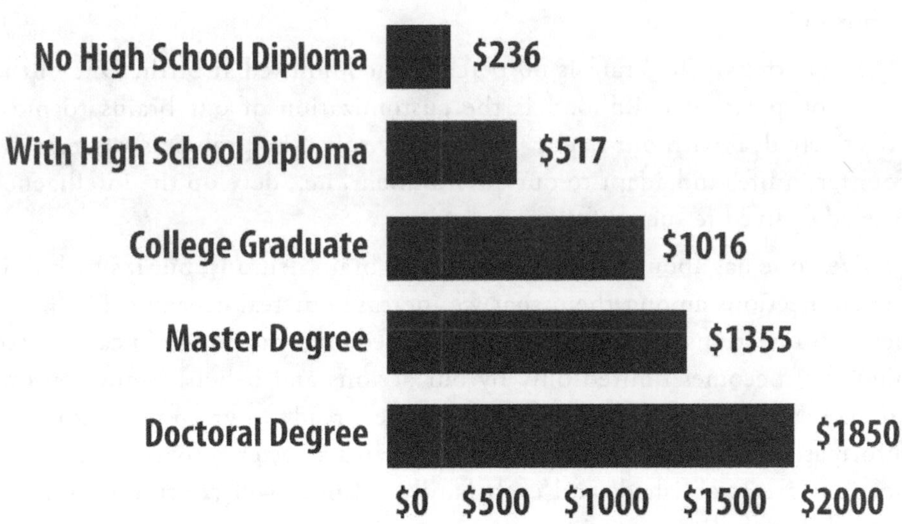

- Individuals with a high school diploma will earn more than double what someone without one will.
- A college degree almost doubles the income possibilities of someone with just a high school diploma.

Higher education or training increases income opportunities, and over a lifetime, just a 10 point increase in IQ may mean as much as an extra million dollars of income or more! A higher IQ enables individuals to reach nearly any goal. Of course, success involves more than IQ. Achievement, motivation, time-management, good use of resources, success habits, and effective strategies are imperative. Although the main objective of IQ Boosters is to increase intelligence, many of the ideas and activities also help build these other essential qualities.

Increase Brain Capacity

By providing your children enriched experiences at home, positive improvements in their developing brains will result. Even physical changes take place as they interact with their environment and engage in learning opportunities.

By providing your children enriched experiences at home, positive improvements in their developing brains will result. Physical changes take place as they interact with their environment and engage in learning opportunities.

The cortex of the brain is 80 percent uncommitted at birth. One of the major purposes of childhood is the customization of our brains to most effectively deal with our needs, successfully solve the problems we may encounter in life, and adapt to our environment, i.e., develop the intelligence needed to live life successfully.

Everyone has about the same number of brain neurons, but it's by building connections among them that we increase our real capacity. The number of connections we may make is unlimited, and the potential capacity of our brain becomes limited only by our actions and beliefs. Brain neurons are like eager hands with outstretched fingers ready to grasp new ideas and information. As your family participates in IQ Booster activities, new connections are established, and each family member will continuously grow toward their fullest potential.

Tools Increase Natural Abilities

YOU PLUS TOOLS EQUALS "WOW!"

Tools enable us to achieve results beyond our natural abilities. It's easy to see this in history. Consider how tools, such as the wheel, books, movable type, the arch, steel, steam power, automobiles, airplanes, computers smartphones, and the Internet have made huge differences in what we can do and accomplish.

Before 1830, an experienced tailor could sew about thirty stitches a minute. In that year, the first sewing machine was invented. Though still primitive by today's standards, it was capable of two hundred stitches a minute. The tailor's power to accomplish a desired task increased over six times. With modern sewing machines, that power has been magnified many times more.

Some of the greatest tools in history have been in the form of ideas, such as the alphabet, writing, the use of the zero, the decimal number system, the equal sign, the power of algebra and physics, the concept of self-esteem, positive thinking, and powerful memory techniques.

Many tools can dramatically boost effective intelligence. Every new IQ boosting tool you and your family use in your own lives will dramatically increase your effective intelligence and abilities.

Increase Success by Leveraging IQ

Using a lever, power may be exerted beyond the normal human capacity. Using the same principle, leverage your IQ. Increase your thinking power by 20 percent simply by verbalizing your thoughts. People tend to talk to themselves as they try to solve difficult problems. This is why a problem is sometimes solved right in the middle of an attempt to explain it to someone else.

Language helps us focus, and since language is based on logic, gaps in our thinking become evident and relationships between elements of the problem become clear when we talk it out. Our natural ability may be leveraged by about 20 percent just by verbalizing our thoughts. A starting IQ of 100 leveraged by 20 percent would operate as a 120 IQ.

LEVERAGE IQ BY 20 PERCENT

90 IQ becomes an effective 108 IQ
100 IQ becomes an effective 120 IQ
110 IQ becomes an effective 132 IQ
120 IQ becomes an effective 144 IQ
130 IQ becomes an effective 156 IQ

LEVERAGE IQ BY 30 PERCENT

90 IQ becomes an effective 117 IQ
100 IQ becomes an effective 130 IQ
110 IQ becomes an effective 143 IQ
120 IQ becomes an effective 156 IQ
130 IQ becomes an effective 169 IQ

Some ways to leverage areas of your IQ are even more dramatic. The average person forgets more than 75 percent of what they learn within the first 24 hours of exposure. Simple leverage techniques may prevent this costly loss and assure more complete retention. For each area of intelligence, IQ Boosters will show you how to use tools and strategies that immediately increase effective or leveraged intelligence, while other developmental methods gradually increase basic intelligence itself.

An Intelligence Support System

Intelligence reaches its full potential by being part of an enriched support system. Have other people with whom you share mutual interests and participate in learning projects. Ask and answer questions, give and receive help, show interest, and give as well as receive positive encouragement — these are all very valuable. Choose a quiet place to study, access to information from books, reference materials, computers, iPads, the Internet and other aids, and the means to participate in other learning opportunities and experiences outside the family.

Good Nutrition & Physical Fitness

Good nutrition is of special importance during pregnancy and the first months of childhood because it can affect the physical development of the brain and nervous system. But at all ages, it is imperative that we eat properly and exercise regularly. Consider about 8 points of IQ being directly related to good nutrition and health.

Model What You Want Your Children to Do

One of the easiest and most efficient ways to learn is to imitate someone else, especially if that person is important in your life. As a parent, do those things that will increase your intelligence and potential for success, and you will provide a positive path for your children to follow.

Recognize & Nurture Talents Early

One of the most rewarding experiences in life is discovering and developing our children's talents and our own talents. *Roots of Success* by Cynthia Pincus Russell describes the need for a three-fold parental commitment.

- Expect greatness to unfold as your child grows up.

- Be intensely involved in your child's development of abilities and talents, especially in the early years.

- Show early recognition and enthusiastic support for your child's emerging special gifts, talents, and interests.

Intelligence Tests

Observing your child doing the activities in *IQ Boosters* will give you a better idea of their current strengths and weaknesses. It may be that your child has been tested at school, and you may already have a summary of their strong and weak IQ areas.

Each *IQ Skill Section* in *IQ Boosters* refers you to the most widely used intelligence tests available today that test those areas of intelligence. They include the *Wechsler Intelligence Tests (WISC)*, the *Stanford-Binet Intelligence Test,* the *Slosson Intelligence Test,* the *Detroit Tests of Learning Aptitude,*

Howard Gardner's multiple intelligences, and others. This enables you to easily use any test information that may be available for your child and help you initiate the most effective ways to promote their success.

The basic organization of *IQ Boosters* relates most to the *Wechsler Intelligence Tests for Children and Adults*. The children's version is often referred to as *WISC*.

- *WISC* is the most widely used test in the United States for assessing individual learning abilities.

- Much of the research on the factors that influence intelligence refers to *WISC*.

- *WISC* is divided into sub-skills that cover most of the areas recognized as important parts of intelligence.

- *WISC* is commonly used in schools to evaluate student strengths and weaknesses in learning abilities and is a primary screening tool to determine if children qualify for various gifted and learning disability programs. Using *IQ Boosters*, parents can build on their children's identified strengths and overcome any weaknesses.

Consider the following graph of one child's *WISC* test results. The bars represent relative strengths and weaknesses. A scaled score of 10 would be considered average for a child that age; above 10 indicates above average performance; scores below 10 indicate below average performance. If this were your child's graph, what would you want to do? With *IQ Boosters,* you decide which activities are needed to strengthen the lower rated areas.

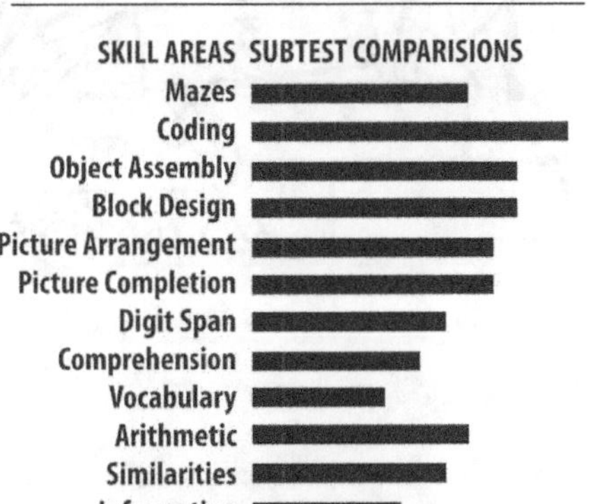

Learning Disabilities

It is important to identify learning disabilities early and correct them as soon as possible in your child's IQ development. Corrective action is important because children, and even adults, often avoid interactions involving a perceived weak area, naturally leading to those skills becoming even weaker. Someone who feels inadequate in general knowledge may shy away from asking questions for fear of revealing their *supposed* ignorance. Thinking they might be weak in short-term memory, a person may simply count on others for reminders and not go through the very processes that build memory skills. We all know people who consider themselves poor in math, thus shunning anything involving numbers.

Even if your child doesn't have the opportunity to take an intelligence test every two or three years as a checkup, observe first-hand how they are doing in each IQ area as your family participates in fun and stimulating *IQ Booster* activities.

IQ Development for Mature Adults

The need for IQ development and stimulation for young children is apparent, which makes it easy to forget that older individuals may benefit from the same IQ boosting activities.

Soon after birth, a child's brain may discard billions of brain neurons because it, evidently, considers them of no use in their current environment. We take notice because it's easy to see dramatic results from what we *do* to help them grow and learn.

But we might forget or not fully realize the need for continued IQ development for ourselves as we age. There is a decided decline in the average scores of tests which have been administered to more mature individuals. At one time, we considered the loss of intelligence to be the natural result of growing older—after the ripe old age of twenty! We now know this is due to many people ceasing to learn, grow, and *exercise* their brains in their senior years.

The average person past fifty begins to lose about 20 percent of their brain neurons. This reminds us of the young child throwing away brain neurons that are not being used. Instead of subjecting ourselves to this type of deterioration, and even to help avoid effects from dementia and other brain ailments, let us use those neurons and continue to make new connections, enabling us to continue life with a growing sense of richness and fulfillment. If seniors continue to develop intelligence and talents, they will fulfill the basic psychological need to share what they have learned, as well as be a part of helping younger loved ones find their own fulfillment and joy in life.

PLANNING GUIDE

These Planning Guides are provided to help you plan your weekly and monthly activities. Use them as a quick reference guide and check off the activities as you complete them. Especially note your favorites.

VERBAL INFORMATION & ALERTNESS

IQ SKILL 1
VERBAL INFORMATION & ALERTNESS
ACTIVITIES

- [ ] 1. Make It a Challenge
- [ ] 2. Weekly Co-Planning Meetings
- [ ] 3. Look-It-Up Habit
- [ ] 4. Long-Term Memory
- [ ] 5. Encourage Questions
- [ ] 6. Question & Answer Bulletin Board
- [ ] 7. Question & Answer Nights
- [ ] 8. Question & Answer Books
- [ ] 9. Cultural Literacy Books
- [ ] 10. Post a World Map
- [ ] 11. History Timelines
- [ ] 12. Interesting Topics
- [ ] 13. Hobbies, Talents, & Interests
- [ ] 14. Family Dinners
- [ ] 15. Five-Minute Daily Drills
- [ ] 16. Quality TV & Media
- [ ] 17. Quotes
- [ ] 18. This Day in History
- [ ] 20. Holiday Bulletin Board
- [ ] 21. Hero of the Month
- [ ] 22. Teach to Learn
- [ ] 23. Watch the News Together
- [ ] 24. The Newspaper
- [ ] 25. Read Something Interesting Every Day
- [ ] 26. Talk About What You Read
- [ ] 27. Follow Interesting News Stories

- [ ] 28. Read with a Pencil
- [ ] 29. Subject of the Month
- [ ] 30. An Experience Table
- [ ] 31. Exact Words
- [ ] 32. Reading & TV Ratio
- [ ] 33. School Textbooks
- [ ] 34. Basic Facts Challenges
- [ ] 35. Become an Expert at Research
- [ ] 36. Library & Online Research
- [ ] 37. Yellow Pages Field Trips
- [ ] 38. Show & Tell
- [ ] 39. Learn from Others' Experiences and Interests
- [ ] 40. Interesting Scrapbooks
- [ ] 41. Special Posters
- [ ] 42. Five-Minute Lessons
- [ ] 43. Memory Cards
- [ ] 44. Famous People
- [ ] 45. Extended Family Learning Letters
- [ ] 46. Learning on Trips
- [ ] 47. Pure (Uninterrupted) Reading Time
- [ ] 48. The Double Method for Reading Speed
- [ ] 49. Mind Maps of Articles or Book Chapters
- [ ] 50. Write in the Margins
- [ ] 51. Mental & Physical Exercise

GAMES

- [ ] 52. Info Grab
- [ ] 53. Timed Flashcard
- [ ] 54. Flashcard Turnover
- [ ] 55. Information Card Capture

- [ ] 56. Time Hit
- [ ] 57. Information Scan
- [ ] 58. Social Studies & Science ABC's
- [ ] 59. Memory Match Games
- [ ] 60. Chain Reaction
- [ ] 61. Biography Rummy
- [ ] 62. Presidential Line-up
- [ ] 63. Presidential Match-up
- [ ] 64. Presidential Claims
- [ ] 65. PicFacts
- [ ] 66. Bulletin Board Question Cards Draw
- [ ] 67. Around the World with Facts
- [ ] 68. Historical Events Line-up
- [ ] 69. Fact-a-Day Strings
- [ ] 70. Who or What Event Am I?
- [ ] 71. Add-a-Fact
- [ ] 72. Information Bingo
- [ ] 73. Information Checkers
- [ ] 74. Scramble

NOTES

____

____

____

____

____

____

____

____

ORGANIZE, GENERALIZE, & CATEGORIZE

IQ SKILL 2
ORGANIZE, GENERALIZE, & CATEGORIZE
ACTIVITIES

- [ ] 1. Make It a Challenge
- [ ] 2. Weekly Co-Planning Meetings
- [ ] 3. Daily Planning & Thinking Time
- [ ] 4. Apply Quotes in Your Life
- [ ] 5. Categories from Online Searches
- [ ] 6. Goals
- [ ] 7. Family Activity Time Agendas & Topics
- [ ] 8. Budgeting
- [ ] 9. Categorize To-Do Lists
- [ ] 10. A Place for Everything
- [ ] 11. Comparisons & Contrasts
- [ ] 12. Connect New Information to Old
- [ ] 13. Metaphors, Analogies, & Stories
- [ ] 14. Discuss Proverbs
- [ ] 15. Pencils Help You Think
- [ ] 16. Visual-Aid Tools
- [ ] 17. Thought-Sharing
- [ ] 18. Retracing Conclusions
- [ ] 19. Collections
- [ ] 20. The Other Side
- [ ] 21. Category Scrapbooks
- [ ] 22. Family & Online Resources
- [ ] 23. Word Lists
- [ ] 24. Word Sorts
- [ ] 25. Memory Nights
- [ ] 26. Refrigerator Door Challenges
- [ ] 27. Computer or Device Databases
- [ ] 28. School-Learning Connects to Life
- [ ] 29. Five-Sentence Summaries

GAMES

NOTES

MENTAL MATH

Copyright 2018 Brent R. Evans

IQ SKILL 3
MENTAL MATH
ACTIVITIES

- [ ] 1. Make It a Challenge
- [ ] 2. Weekly Co-Planning Meetings
- [ ] 3. Memory Squares to Master Math Skills
- [ ] 4. Math Skills Record Sheets
- [ ] 5. Family Financial Success
- [ ] 6. Budgeting
- [ ] 7. Personal Financial Accounts
- [ ] 8. Development & Education Budget
- [ ] 9. Memorize Personal Statistics
- [ ] 10. Allowances & Bonuses
- [ ] 11. Money Requests Must Be Specific
- [ ] 12. Match Funds for Personal Goals
- [ ] 13. A Family Business
- [ ] 14. A Family Bank
- [ ] 15. Estimate Shopping Totals
- [ ] 16. Coupons
- [ ] 17. Recycle
- [ ] 18. Good Buying Strategies
- [ ] 19. Math in Meal Planning
- [ ] 20. Utilities Savings
- [ ] 21. Discuss Math Homework Regularly
- [ ] 22. Discuss Math at Mealtime
- [ ] 23. Use Math in Discussing the News
- [ ] 24. Math Story Problems
- [ ] 25. Track Your Car's Miles Per Gallon
- [ ] 25. Mental Arithmetic
- [ ] 27. Time Concepts

Master Math Facts, Tricks, & Strategies

- ☐ 58. Number Detective Trick
- ☐ 59. Card Identification Trick
- ☐ 60. Square 90s the Fast Way
- ☐ 61. Square Two-Place Numbers Ending in 5
- ☐ 62. Square Numbers Formed by 9s
- ☐ 63. Multiplying Two-Place Numbers Ending in 5 When the Sum of 10s' Digits is Even
- ☐ 64. Multiplying Two-Place Numbers Ending in 5 When the Sum of 10s' Digits is Odd
- ☐ 65. Multiply Two-Place Numbers by 11
- ☐ 66. Multiply Long Numbers by 11
- ☐ 67. Complement Method of Multiplying
- ☐ 68. Supplement Method of Multiplying
- ☐ 69. Check Multiplication: Cast Out 9s
- ☐ 70. Check Division: Cast Out 9s
- ☐ 71. Predict Remainders
- ☐ 72. Add Simple Fractions
- ☐ 73. Subtract Simple Fractions
- ☐ 74. Divide Simple Fractions
- ☐ 75. Numbers Divisible by 2
- ☐ Numbers Divisible by 3
- ☐ Numbers Divisible by 4
- ☐ Numbers Divisible by 5
- ☐ Numbers Divisible by 6
- ☐ Numbers Divisible by 8
- ☐ Numbers Divisible by 9
- ☐ Numbers Divisible by 10
- ☐ Numbers Divisible by 12
- ☐ 76. Find the Day of the Week for Any Date
- ☐ 77. Place Value Puzzler
- ☐ 78. Total of the Week Addition

☐ 79. Calendar Addition

☐ 80. Generate Number Patterns

☐ 81. The Answer is Always 18

☐ 82. The Answer is Always 37

☐ 83. Odd or Even Hands

☐ 84. Multiply by 5

☐ Multiply by 50

☐ Multiply by 25

GAMES

☐ 85. Calendar Regular Math Game Nights

☐ 86. Got It!

☐ 87. Thirty-Seconds Card Game

☐ 88. Mental Math Competition

☐ 89. Plus & Minus Bingo with Cards

☐ 90. Bean Bag Throw

☐ 91. Speed: Regular & Modified

☐ 92. Speed: Addition & Subtraction

☐ 93. Small Yacht

☐ 94. Timed Races

☐ 95. Multiple Targets

☐ 96. Number Connections

☐ 97. Checkerboard Golf

☐ 98. Green Light

☐ 99. Checkerboard Battle

☐ 100. Dice Elevator

☐ 101. Dice Multiplication Cross-out

☐ 102. Total Poker

☐ 103. Decimal Dice

☐ 104. Edge of the Cliff

NOTES

____

____

____

____

____

____

____

____

____

____

____

____

____

____

____

____

VOCABULARY

SAILING MADE EASY
IT'S SIMPLE ...
WHEN YOU'RE READY TO TACK, YOU PUSH THE TILLER LEEWARD. YOU NEED, OF COURSE, TO KNOW IF THE WIND IS BLOWING OVER YOUR STARBOARD OR PORT SIDE !

IQ SKILL 4
VOCABULARY
ACTIVITIES

- [ ] 1. Make It a Challenge
- [ ] 2. Weekly Co-Planning Meetings
- [ ] 3. Personal Vocabulary Program
- [ ] 4. Memory Squares
- [ ] 5. Systematic Review Plan
- [ ] 6. Magazines, Books, Recordings & Apps
- [ ] 7. Character Trait Words & Quotes
- [ ] 8. Word-a-Day Calendar
- [ ] 9. Make Vocabulary Questions a Habit
- [ ] 10. Basic Words for Each Subject
- [ ] 11. Vocabulary Learning Nets
- [ ] 12. Browse Through the Dictionary or Glossary
- [ ] 13. Five New Words Every Day
- [ ] 14. Synonym Cluster Display
- [ ] 15. Vocabulary Bookmarks
- [ ] 16. Expressive Bulletin Boards
- [ ] 17. Attend Library Programs
- [ ] 18. Word Origins
- [ ] 19. Word Pictures
- [ ] 20. Vocabulary Learning Wall
- [ ] 21. Bathroom Mirror
- [ ] 22. Personal Target Chart
- [ ] 23. Computer Dictionary & Thesaurus
- [ ] 24. Vocabulary Place Mats
- [ ] 25. Vocabulary Posters
- [ ] 26. Vocabulary Recordings

NOTES

PRACTICAL LIVING & GOOD JUDGMENT
Copyright 2018 Brent R. Evans

IQ SKILL 5
PRACTICAL LIVING & GOOD JUDGMENT
ACTIVITIES

☐ 1. Make It a Challenge

☐ 2. Weekly Co-Planning Meetings

☐ 3. Values & Goals

☐ 4. Daily Personal & Family Planning

☐ 5. Favorite Quote of the Week

☐ 6. Family Project-of-the-Month

☐ 7. Organizing Projects

☐ 8. Learning How

☐ 9. Problem Awareness

☐ 10. Roles & Responsibilities

☐ 11. Family Activity Time Planner

☐ 12. Good Ideas

☐ 13. Use a Time Management Planner

☐ 14. Personal History Questions

☐ 15. Family Journal Dialogue

☐ 16. Family Constitution

☐ 17. Discuss Reasons Behind the News

☐ 18. Cultural Literacy: The Internet & Libraries

☐ 19. Share Problem Experiences

☐ 20. The Whys of Rules & Laws

☐ 21. Social Events

☐ 22. Interesting Questions

☐ 23. Good Books

☐ 24. Guests

☐ 25. Fables and Folklore

☐ 26. Scout Manuals

- ☐ 27. Why You Do Things
- ☐ 28. Quality Job Training
- ☐ 29. Family Improvements
- ☐ 30. The Reason Why
- ☐ 31. Cause & Effect
- ☐ 32. Right & Wrong Behavior
- ☐ 33. "What-Would-You-Do?" Nights
- ☐ 34. The Importance of Asking Why
- ☐ 35. A Question a Day
- ☐ 36. Traffic Laws
- ☐ 37. The United States Constitution
- ☐ 38. Law
- ☐ 39. Poisons & Antidotes
- ☐ 40. Fire Prevention & Safety
- ☐ 41. Drugs
- ☐ 42. Study Etiquette
- ☐ 43. Care for Pets
- ☐ 44. Family Pulitzer Prizes
- ☐ 45. Diseases
- ☐ 46. Physical Fitness
- ☐ 47. Food Quality
- ☐ 48. First Aid

GAMES

- ☐ 49. Guess What They Will Do
- ☐ 50. Suggestion Sentence Hangman
- ☐ 51. Situation Skits
- ☐ 52. Pause and Predict
- ☐ 53. Choices Count
- ☐ 54. Alternate Endings
- ☐ 55. The Best Advice
- ☐ 56. Name That Proverb

- [ ] 57. Wisdom from Around the World
- [ ] 58. Grocery Challenge
- [ ] 59. Core Values

NOTES

POWER POSTER 6

LISTEN & REMEMBER

Copyright 2018 Brent R. Evans

IQ SKILL 6
LISTEN & REMEMBER
ACTIVITIES

- [ ] 1. Make It a Challenge
- [ ] 2. Weekly Co-Planning Meetings
- [ ] 3. Calendaring & Planning
- [ ] 4. Important Learning Events Daily
- [ ] 5. Remember Names
- [ ] 6. Family Job Descriptions
- [ ] 7. Daily Job Announcements
- [ ] 8. How-to Memory Books
- [ ] 9. Memorize Quotes
- [ ] 10. Memorize Something New Every Day
- [ ] 11. Calendar Coordination
- [ ] 12. How to Take Telephone Messages
- [ ] 13. The Gift of Being Fully Heard
- [ ] 14. Expect a Good Memory
- [ ] 15. Do Not Reward Forgetting
- [ ] 16. Make Requests Through the Day
- [ ] 17. The Listening Position
- [ ] 18. Limit Repeating Directions
- [ ] 19. Touch—Watch—Repeat
- [ ] 20. Train for & Expect Quality Work
- [ ] 21. Phone Home & Delegate
- [ ] 22. Story Questions
- [ ] 23. Oral Shopping Lists
- [ ] 24. Memory Essentials
- [ ] 25. Memorize by Erasing
- [ ] 26. Keyword Memorizing
- [ ] 27. Jokes, Stories, & Poetry Nights

☐ 28. TV Program & Movie Sharing

☐ 29. Record & Replay Good Programs

☐ 30. Encourage Gap Filling

☐ 31. Have Children Get Needed Information

☐ 32. Words in a Row Before You Go

☐ 33. Learn Songs & Parts

☐ 34. Memorize & Sing Jingles

☐ 35. Paired Interviews

☐ 36. Memory Aerobics

☐ 37. Take Notes

☐ 38. Recorded Messages Instead of Letters

☐ 39. Listen to & Discuss the News

☐ 40. Subscribe & Listen to Interesting Podcasts

☐ 41. Audiobooks

☐ 42. Learn Useful Phrases in Another Language

GAMES

☐ 43. Ghost

☐ 44. Fun with Tongue Twisters

☐ 45. Finger Plays, Rhymes, & Stories

☐ 46. News Story Chains

☐ 47. The Missing Card

☐ 48. Prize Telephone Numbers

☐ 49. First to Reach 100 Race

☐ 59. Word Turnover

☐ 51. Sentence Challenges

☐ 52. Direction Duels

☐ 53. Bouncing a Ball

☐ 54. Direction Dares

☐ 55. Tapping Game

☐ 56. Word Bank

☐ 57. Back Talk

- [ ] 58. Double-Trouble Spelling Bee
- [ ] 59. Morse Code
- [ ] 60. Memory List Scavenger Hunt
- [ ] 61. Right Answer Race
- [ ] 62. Who Stole the Cookies?
- [ ] 63. Snap to It
- [ ] 64. Someone Says
- [ ] 65. I Went to the Store
- [ ] 66. Draw This Picture
- [ ] 67. Who Sir? I Sir?
- [ ] 68. One Word Longer
- [ ] 69. This is a What?
- [ ] 70. The Name Game
- [ ] 71. Digit Test Challenges
- [ ] 72. Lip Reading
- [ ] 73. Building Target Words
- [ ] 74. Sentence Repeats
- [ ] Four-Word Sentences
- [ ] Five-Word Sentences
- [ ] Six-Word Sentences 208
- [ ] Seven-Word Sentences
- [ ] Eight-Word Sentences
- [ ] Nine-Word Sentences
- [ ] Ten-Word Sentences
- [ ] Eleven-Word Sentences
- [ ] Twelve-Word Sentences
- [ ] Thirteen-Word Sentences
- [ ] Fourteen-Word Sentences
- [ ] Fifteen-Word Sentences
- [ ] Sixteen-Word Sentences
- [ ] Seventeen-Word Sentences
- [ ] Eighteen-Word Sentences

VISUAL INFORMATION & ALERTNESS

IQ SKILLS 7
VISUAL INFORMATION & ALERTNESS
ACTIVITIES

- [ ] 1. Make It a Challenge
- [ ] 2. Weekly Co-Planning Meetings
- [ ] 3. Draw What You See
- [ ] 4. Sketch Your Ideas
- [ ] 5. Names & Faces
- [ ] 6. Memorize Illustrations
- [ ] 7. Weekly Visual Reviews
- [ ] 8. Draw What You Want to Remember
- [ ] 9. Observation Walks
- [ ] 10. On My Way, I Saw
- [ ] 11. Magnifying Glass
- [ ] 12. Observation Corner
- [ ] 13. Sherlock Holmes' Stories
- [ ] 14. Observation Questions
- [ ] 15. Observing & Learning About Ants
- [ ] 16. Bird Watching
- [ ] 17. Aquariums
- [ ] 18. Penicillin Mold Experiments
- [ ] 19. Talk About Pictures You See
- [ ] 20. Photo Talks
- [ ] 21. Draw Memories
- [ ] 22. Learn to Cook: Recipes
- [ ] 23. Family Resources Picture Tours
- [ ] 24. Read & Illustrate
- [ ] 25. Learning Posters
- [ ] 26. Skimming Reading Material
- [ ] 27. Hobby Collections
- [ ] 28. Draw What You See on a Trip

☐ 29. Trip Souvenir Box

☐ 30. Use a Card to Help You Focus

☐ 31. Paint-by-Number

☐ 32. Collect Leaf Rubbings or Prints

☐ 33. Double- and Triple-check Schoolwork

☐ 34. Take Photo or Video Field Trips

☐ 35. Watch Art Programs

☐ 36. Watch Science Programs

☐ 37. Establish a Living Scrapbook

☐ 38 . Use Visual Aids

☐ 39. Practice Quality Food Shopping

☐ 40. Perform Magic Tricks

☐ 41. Learn Sports Signals

☐ 42. Manual Alphabet & Communication System

☐ 43. Compound Word Pictures

☐ 44. Match Buttons

☐ 45. Play Musical Instruments & Sing Together

☐ 46. Say What You See & Are Doing

GAMES

☐ 47. Magic Finger

☐ 48. First to Find

☐ 49. Money Magic

☐ 50. Egyptian War

☐ 51. State Scan

☐ 52. Face Scan

☐ 53. Object Scan

☐ 54. Guess Which

☐ 55. Day of the Week Visual Memories

☐ 56. Play Back

☐ 57. Scenes from History

☐ 58. Map Drawing from Memory

- [ ] 59. Pictorial Maps
- [ ] 60. Close-Up
- [ ] 61. Word Search Puzzles
- [ ] 62. Write Rebus Stories
- [ ] 63. Popularity Contests
- [ ] 64. Traveling Alphabet Races
- [ ] 65. Word-Parts Card Game
- [ ] 66. Travel Bingo
- [ ] 67. Dot-to-Dot Books
- [ ] 68. Famous People Photos
- [ ] 69. Missing Letters
- [ ] 70. Patterns
- [ ] 71. Word Completions
- [ ] 72. Letter Combination Searches
- [ ] 73. Miniature Hide & Seek
- [ ] 74. Dominoes
- [ ] 75. Crossfire
- [ ] 76. Find It in Illustrations
- [ ] 77. Draw & Find
- [ ] 78. Imaginary Hide & Seek
- [ ] 79. Jigsaw Puzzles
- [ ] 80. Word & Phrase Flash Game
- [ ] 81. Fingerprinting
- [ ] 82. Drawings
- [ ] 83. Animal Chairs
- [ ] 84. Roll the Marble in the Bowl
- [ ] 85. Frustration
- [ ] 86. Flip-Card Action Scenes
- [ ] 87. Grocery Replacement Games
- [ ] 88. Hidden Letters Search
- [ ] 89. Hidden Pictures
- [ ] 90. Runway Model

CAUSE & EFFECT IN SOCIAL SITUATIONS

Copyright 2018 Brent R. Evans

IQ SKILL 8
CAUSE & EFFECT IN SOCIAL SITUATIONS
ACTIVITIES

- [ ] 1. Make It a Challenge
- [ ] 2.Weekly Co-Planning Meetings
- [ ] 3. Read a Quote a Day
- [ ] 4. Success Habits
- [ ] 5. Prioritizing & Planning Your Time
- [ ] 6. Planning Projects
- [ ] 7. Job Descriptions
- [ ] 8. Recipes
- [ ] 9. Theme for the Day
- [ ] 10. Beginning of the Day Previews
- [ ] 11. End of the Day Reviews
- [ ] 12. Sharing Personal Stories
- [ ] 13. Family or Friend Slumber Parties
- [ ] 14. Read & Discuss the News
- [ ] 15. Read & Discuss History Books
- [ ] 16. Watch & Discuss Good Movies
- [ ] 17. TV Stop & Talk
- [ ] 18. Comic Strips
- [ ] 19. Unfinished Stories
- [ ] 20. Draw Cartoon Stories
- [ ] 21. Book Reviews
- [ ] 22. Book Sharing After Dinner
- [ ] 23. Identify Behavior Patterns
- [ ] 24. Draw What Happened
- [ ] 25. Dream Talks
- [ ] 26. Role-Play Problems

- [ ] 27. Family Advice Column
- [ ] 28. Parties & Family Entertainment
- [ ] 29. Skill Demonstrations
- [ ] 30. Planning Trips or Family Outings
- [ ] 31. Personal Development Books
- [ ] 32. Job Resumes
- [ ] 33. Timelines
- [ ] 34. Puppets
- [ ] 35. Family Documentaries
- [ ] 36. Personal Models of the World

GAMES

- [ ] 37. Picture Replays
- [ ] 38. Create Stories from Pictures
- [ ] 39. Ad Stories
- [ ] 40. Cave Drawings
- [ ] 41. Finger Plays & Action Stories
- [ ] 42. Random Object Stories
- [ ] 43. Joke & Cartoon Skits
- [ ] 44. Emotion Word Skits
- [ ] 45. Pantomime Pictionary
- [ ] 46. Stringing Necklaces
- [ ] 47. Beginnings, Middles, & Endings

NOTES

DESIGN & CONSTRUCT WITH A MODEL
MODEL PLANE
DIRECTIONS
GLUE

IQ SKILL 9
DESIGN & CONSTRUCT WITH A MODEL
ACTIVITIES

- [ ] 1. Make It a Challenge
- [ ] 2. Weekly Co-Planning Meetings
- [ ] 3. Daily Planning Time
- [ ] 4. Projects
- [ ] 5. How Things Are Constructed
- [ ] 6. Addresses & Directions
- [ ] 7. House Memories
- [ ] 8. Mental Gymnastics
- [ ] 9. Seeing Through the Crosshairs
- [ ] 10. Orient with Maps
- [ ] 11. Practice Visual Thinking
- [ ] 12. Newspaper Visuals
- [ ] 13. Family Library or Online Visuals
- [ ] 14. Flow Charts
- [ ] 15. How Things Work
- [ ] 16. Breaking Problems Down to Size
- [ ] 17. Mind-Mapping Techniques
- [ ] 18. Copying Written Material
- [ ] 19. Visual Overload
- [ ] 20. Shape Sight-Seeing
- [ ] 21. Love Geometry
- [ ] 22. Kaleidoscope
- [ ] 23. Balsa Wood Gliders
- [ ] 24. Paper Airplanes
- [ ] 25. Gift Wrapping
- [ ] 26. Kites

☐ 27. Balloon Animals, Toys, & Shapes

☐ 28. Woodworking

☐ 29. Computer Activities

☐ 30. Science Programs

☐ 31. Create House Plans

☐ 32. Weaving

☐ 33. Invention of the Month

☐ 34. Weather Station

☐ 35. Know Your Tools & Materials

☐ 36. Home Repairs & Maintenance

☐ 37. Mosaics

☐ 38. Macramé

☐ 39. Bike Repairs & Maintenance

☐ 40. Your Car

☐ 41. Auto Emergency Tool Kit

☐ 42. Construction Field Trips

☐ 43. Paper-Folding

☐ 44. Assembly Required

☐ 45. Indian Beadwork

☐ 46. Graph Paper Weaving Designs

☐ 47. Perspectives

GAMES

☐ 48. Design Squares Challenge

☐ 49. Graph Paper Designs

☐ 50. Dot Designs

☐ 51. Following Directions Challenges

☐ 52. Mirror Drawing

☐ 53. Draw What I Say

☐ 54. Mind Pictures

- [ ] 55. Drawing in the Air
- [ ] 56. Hole Predictions
- [ ] 57. Mind Traveling
- [ ] 58. Picture Parts
- [ ] 59. Mystery Bag
- [ ] 60. Images in the Clouds
- [ ] 61. Blindfold Drawing
- [ ] 62. Action Rhymes & Verses
- [ ] 63. Actions
- [ ] 64. Vase Faces
- [ ] 65. Half & Half Drawings
- [ ] 66. Gyroscopes
- [ ] 67. No Boundary Tic Tac Toe
- [ ] 68. Scaled Drawing Challenges
- [ ] 69. Intersections
- [ ] 70. Shape Completion Card Game

NOTES

____

____

____

____

____

____

____

____

____

____

DESIGN & CONSTRUCT WITHOUT A MODEL

Copyright 2018 Brent R. Evans

IQ SKILL 10
DESIGN & CONSTRUCT WITHOUT A MODEL
ACTIVITIES

- [ ] 1. Make It a Challenge
- [ ] 2. Weekly Co-Planning Meetings
- [ ] 3. Organize for Success
- [ ] 4. Create, Operate, or Fix Things
- [ ] 5. Frustration Lists
- [ ] 6. Sketching & Capturing Ideas
- [ ] 7. Hands-on Learning
- [ ] 8. Photo Collage
- [ ] 9. The Whole Picture
- [ ] 10. Knowledge Maps
- [ ] 11. Papier Mâché
- [ ] 12. Science Displays & Mobiles

GAMES

- [ ] 13. Animal Puzzle Parts
- [ ] 14. Tangrams
- [ ] 15. Penny Checkers
- [ ] 16. Coin Chess
- [ ] 17. Four-in-a-Row
- [ ] 18. Knight Out
- [ ] 19. Derrah
- [ ] 20. Penny Take-Away
- [ ] 21. Last Line
- [ ] 22. Strategy Pickup
- [ ] 23. Tower of Hanoi
- [ ] 24. Planting Trees Puzzle

- [ ] 25. Dot Puzzles
- [ ] 26. Nickels & Pennies War
- [ ] 27. Coin Attack
- [ ] 28. Countdown
- [ ] 29. Triangle Jump Puzzler
- [ ] 30. Straight Line Heads to Tails
- [ ] 31. Star Slide
- [ ] 32. Nine Men's Morris
- [ ] 33. Fourth Count
- [ ] 34. Heads to Tails (Double Diamonds)
- [ ] 35. Othello
- [ ] 36. Toothpick Problems
- [ ] 37. Up-to-Down Puzzle
- [ ] 38. Jigsaw Puzzles
- [ ] 39. Jigsaw Puzzle Points
- [ ] 40. Jigsaw Puzzle Mix
- [ ] 41. Team Letters
- [ ] 42. Sprouts
- [ ] 43. Computer Games
- [ ] 44. Guess What?
- [ ] 45. Shadow Pictures
- [ ] 46. Golf
- [ ] 47. Billiards
- [ ] 48. Bowling8

NOTES

SEE & REMEMBER

IQ SKILL 11
SEE & REMEMBER
ACTIVITIES

☐ 1. Make It a Challenge
☐ 2. Weekly Co-Planning Meetings
☐ 3. Looking Up Phone Numbers
☐ 4. Names & Faces
☐ 5. Memorize Personal Information
☐ 6. Flip-over Study Technique
☐ 7. Visual Descriptions
☐ 8. Planning & Thinking Time
☐ 9. Copying Things into Your Organizer
☐ 10. Learn to Spell a New Word a Day
☐ 11. See & Repeat
☐ 12. Share What You Saw
☐ 13. Use Mnemonics
☐ 14. Typing
☐ 15. Learn New Communication Systems
☐ 16. Flashlight Morse Code
☐ 17. Drawing Lessons
☐ 18. Look, Turn, and Draw
☐ 19. Computer Spelling Programs
☐ 20. Learn New Dance Steps

GAMES

☐ 21. Memory Card Challenge
☐ 22. Match Makers
☐ 23. What's in the Box?
☐ 24. Picture Duel
☐ 25. Memory Design Card Challenges
☐ 26. Pencil Obstacle Course

- [ ] 27. Look What I See
- [ ] 28. State Race
- [ ] 29. What's Missing?
- [ ] 30. Picture Memory
- [ ] 31. Construction Memory
- [ ] 32. License Plates
- [ ] 33. Phone Book
- [ ] 34. Eyewitness
- [ ] 35. Pencil Attack
- [ ] 36. Target Number
- [ ] 37. Funny Eggs
- [ ] 38. Making Knots
- [ ] 39. Delayed Copycat
- [ ] 40. Find & Circle
- [ ] 41. Challenge to Draw
- [ ] 42. Cross-Out-Letters Puzzles
- [ ] 43. Copy Sentences
- [ ] 44. Sorting Games with Time Limits
- [ ] 45. Tic Tac Toe Code
- [ ] 46. Memory Tic-Tac-Toe
- [ ] 47. Alphabet Codes
- [ ] 48. Reproduce Digit/Designs
- [ ] 49. Changed Hands
- [ ] 50. Turn Around
- [ ] 51. Perjury
- [ ] 52. Room for Change
- [ ] 53. Blindfold Obstacle Course
- [ ] 54. Checkerboard Memory
- [ ] 55. Observation
- [ ] 56. Poison Checkers
- [ ] 57. Morse Code Notes
- [ ] 58. Memory Poker

Other Resources

NOTES

Copyright 2018 Brent R. Evans

IQ SKILL 12
VISUAL MOTOR ABILITIES
ACTIVITIES

- [ ] 1. Make It a Challenge
- [ ] 2. Weekly Co-Planning Meetings
- [ ] 3. Personal & Family Organizer
- [ ] 4. Maps
- [ ] 5. Visual Motor Coordination Practice Sheets
- [ ] 6. Interesting Things to See
- [ ] 7. Use Your Finger or Marker While Reading
- [ ] 8. Chalkboard or Whiteboard Drawing
- [ ] 9. Highlight Special Papers
- [ ] 10. Eye-Tracking Exercise
- [ ] 11. Looking Through Your Finger
- [ ] 12. Finger Frames Exercise
- [ ] 13. Eye Landings Exercise
- [ ] 14. Pointing
- [ ] 15. Look & Say Exercise
- [ ] 16. Near & Far Copying Exercises
- [ ] 17. Round Trips Exercise
- [ ] 18. Handing Things from the Side
- [ ] 19. Spotter
- [ ] 20. Visual Arts Drawer
- [ ] 21. Finger Painting

GAMES

- [ ] 22. Pencil Golf
- [ ] 23. Electric Hookups
- [ ] 24. Coin Flip Games
- [ ] 25. Pennies Turnover

- [ ] 26. Circle Words
- [ ] 27. Cut & Paste
- [ ] 28. Bean Bag Tricks
- [ ] 29. Bombs Away
- [ ] 30. Pile-on Checkers
- [ ] 31. Playing Cars
- [ ] 32. Computer- or Player-Made Mazes
- [ ] 33. Dot-to-Dot Activities
- [ ] 34. Coloring Book Tracing
- [ ] 35. Overlapping Pictures
- [ ] 36. Winding Roads
- [ ] 37. Making & Flying Gliders
- [ ] 38. Card Racers
- [ ] 39. Letter Races
- [ ] 40. Blindfold Art
- [ ] 41. Checkerboard Chinese Checkers
- [ ] 42. Ace-to-King Relays
- [ ] 43. Paper Clip Chains
- [ ] 44. Marble Drop & Capture
- [ ] 45. Creative Dots
- [ ] 46. Marble Shootout
- [ ] 47. Paper Chains & Decorations
- [ ] 48. Quick & Careful Cards
- [ ] 49. Three Words to Many
- [ ] 50. Shirt-Buttoning Races
- [ ] 51. Table Croquet
- [ ] 52. Spoons & Beans
- [ ] 53. Table Golf
- [ ] 54. Forgery
- [ ] 55. Domino Trains
- [ ] 56. Letter or Word Races

☐ 57. Penny Cliffhangers

☐ 58. Tents

☐ 59. Waves

☐ 60. Dot Link-Up Game

☐ 62. End-of-the-Line Dot Game

☐ 63. Magic Trick Parties

☐ 64. Nuts & Bolts

Other Resources

NOTES

____

____

____

____

____

____

____

____

____

____

____

____

____

____

CREATIVITY
HAS ANYONE SEEN MY NEW TIE ?
Copyright 2018 Brent R. Evans

IQ SKILL 13
CREATIVITY
ACTIVITIES

- [ ] 1. Make It a Challenge
- [ ] 2. Weekly Co-Planning Meetings
- [ ] 3. Write Your Ideas
- [ ] 4. Regular Planning
- [ ] 5. Goal Planning
- [ ] 6. Subconscious Abilities
- [ ] 7. Deferred Judgment
- [ ] 8. Time & Freedom
- [ ] 9. Write Your Own Quotations
- [ ] 10 Intuition
- [ ] 11. New Idea for the Week
- [ ] 12. Write Valuable Ideas in Your Idea Journal
- [ ] 13. Collect & Share Clever Writings
- [ ] 14. Creative Greeting Cards
- [ ] 15. Recipe of the Month
- [ ] 16. Creative Table Decorations
- [ ] 17. Pancake Fun
- [ ] 18. Invent New Holidays & Traditions
- [ ] 19. Product Improvements
- [ ] 20. Room Arrangements & Decorations
- [ ] 21. New Clothing Ideas
- [ ] 22. Creative Parties
- [ ] 23. Home & Family Improvements
- [ ] 24. Share Dream Experiences
- [ ] 25. Share Daydreams
- [ ] 26. Explore Pretend Conditions

☐ 27. Interesting People

☐ 28. Debate/Switching Sides

☐ 29. New Uses for Common Objects

☐ 30. Read O'Henry Stories

☐ 31. Alternate Decisions

☐ 32. Collect & Share Riddles

☐ 33. Cooperative Bedtime Stories

☐ 34. Humor Variations

☐ 35. Joke Skits

☐ 36. Symbolic Gifts

☐ 37. New Words to Old Songs

☐ 38. Observe Nature

☐ 39. Odds & Ends Art

☐ 40. Rockville

☐ 41. Arts & Crafts for the Month

☐ 42. Silly Sound Posters

☐ 43. Dots & Lines Pictures

☐ 44. Practice Brainstorming

GAMES

☐ 45. Stepping Through an Index Card

☐ 46. Animal & Object Interviews

☐ 47. New Animals

☐ 48. Pun Fun

☐ 49. Word Associations

☐ 50. Letter Brainstorm

☐ 51. Question & Answer Fold-Overs

☐ 52. Attributes

☐ 53. What Are You Doing?

☐ 54. Related Words

- [ ] 55. Make Up Games
- [ ] 56. Story Ball
- [ ] 57. Number Words
- [ ] 58. Ship Exercises
- [ ] 59. Oneupmanship
- [ ] 60. Literal Headline Pictures
- [ ] 61. Slaphappy Talk
- [ ] 62. One Letter at a Time
- [ ] 63. Tom Swiftly
- [ ] 64. Make Up a New Language
- [ ] 65. Letter Rearrangements
- [ ] 66. Hidden Animals
- [ ] 67. Proverb Play
- [ ] 68. Silly Perspective Fairy Tales
- [ ] 69. Picture Backs
- [ ] 70. What Am I from What Point of View?
- [ ] 71. Creating Puppets
- [ ] 72. Win or Lose Checkers
- [ ] 73. News Perspectives
- [ ] 74. Word Mix-ups
- [ ] 75. Naught-E Game
- [ ] 76. Read 7-Count
- [ ] 77. If Not a Person
- [ ] 78. A Hole in Your Hand
- [ ] 79. Act Like That
- [ ] 80. Fun Lists
- [ ] 81. Let's Pretend
- [ ] 82. Funny People
- [ ] 83. Word Association Chains
- [ ] 84. Game Improvements
- [ ] 85. Collect and Enjoy Puns

NOTES